PIANO SOLO EDITION

Sergei Rachmaninoff

Opus 18

SECOND PIANO CONCERTO

Edited by

ALBERT GAMSE

(Chord Names Included)

PUBLICATIONS

Music Sales America

DISTRIBUTED BY

HAL•LEONARD®
CORPORATION

7777 W. BLUEMOUND RD. P.O. BOX 13819 MILWAUKEE, WI 53213

SERGEI RACHMANINOFF

BORN NOVGOROD, RUSSIA, APRIL 1, 1873
DIED BEVERLY HILLS, CALIF., MARCH 28, 1943

Rachmaninoff, the son of a Russian land-owner, started his musical career at age 9 at the St. Petersburg Conservatory and (three years later) the Moscow Conservatory. Here indeed was a "child prodigy" whose prominence in the music world increased with the passing years.

He was only 20 when he created what was to become one of the most performed pieces of the entire world, the famous PRELUDE IN C SHARP MINOR. Shortly after completing this work, he left Russia permanently, with his wife and two children, and made his home in Paris for several years, then Switzerland, later New York, and (at the time of his death) he was residing in Hollywood, California.

He was constantly on tour. He had gained fame not only as a composer but also as one of the world's most gifted pianists. He wrote three symphonies, four piano concertos (of which the second is the most frequently performed all over the world), and other works destined to take their places alongside the works of the great masters of other centuries.

His Prelude in C Sharp Minor has been rivaled in popularity by the PRELUDE IN G MINOR. Equally familiar are his RHAPSODY ON A THEME BY PAGANINI, HUMOR-ESKE, POLICHINELLE, VALSE IN A, and many other symphonic poems, dances, and piano pieces.

PIANO SOLO EDITION

SECOND PIANO CONCERTO

Sergei Rachmaninoff, Opus 18

INDEX TO PRINCIPAL MOVEMENTS

SECOND PIANO CONCERTO

SERGEI RACHMANINOFF, Op. 18

I

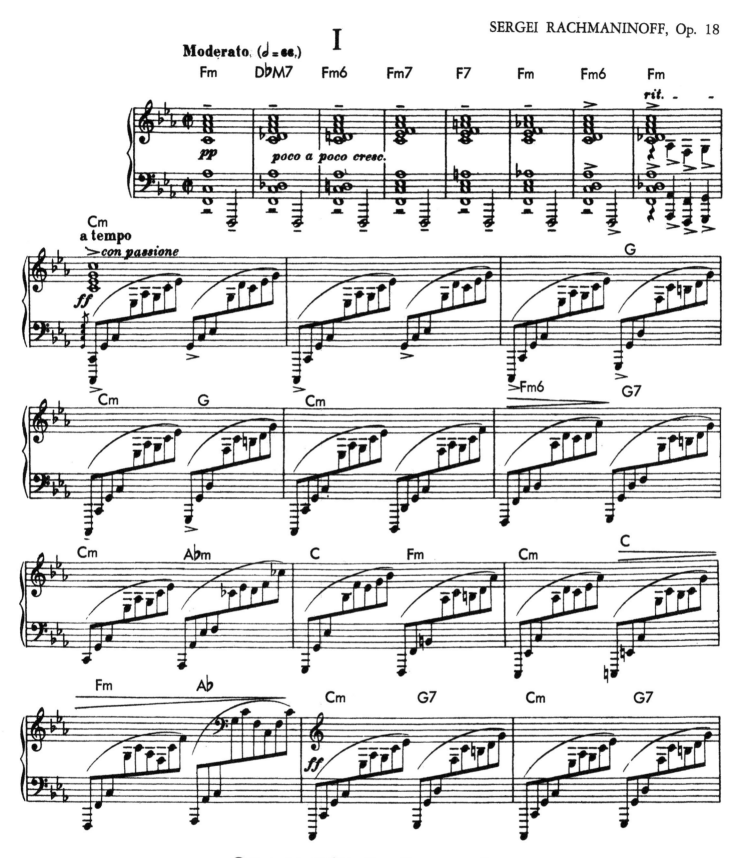

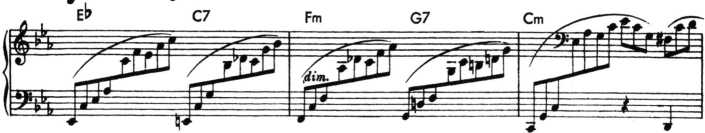

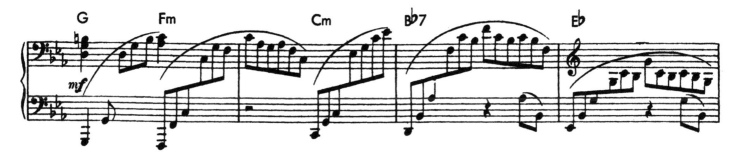

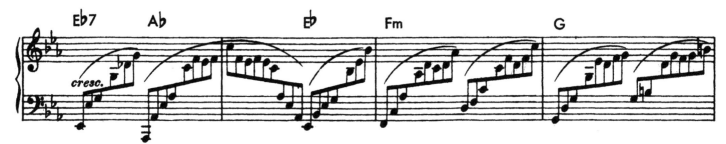

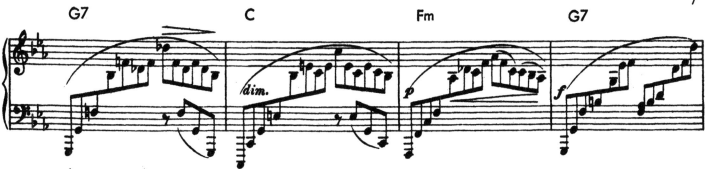

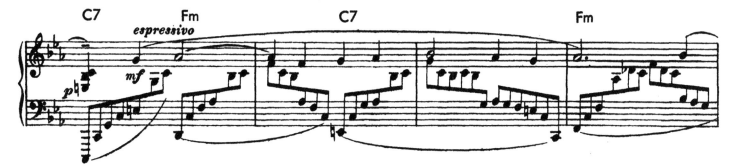

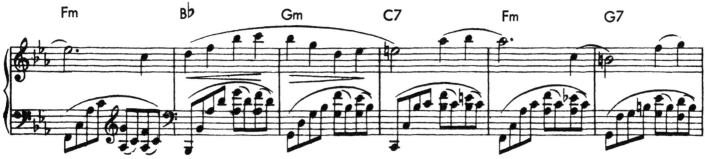

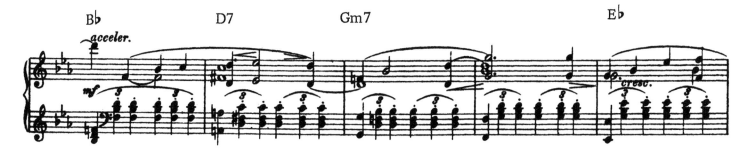

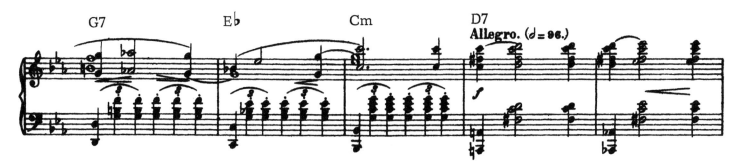

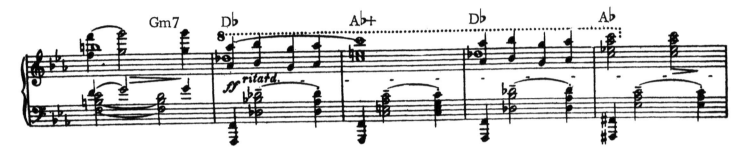

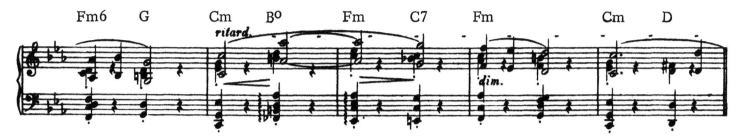

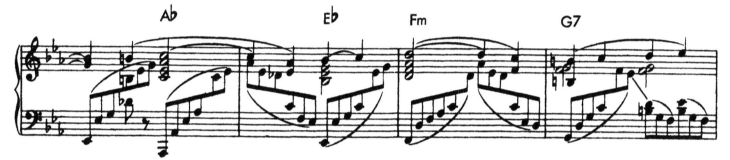

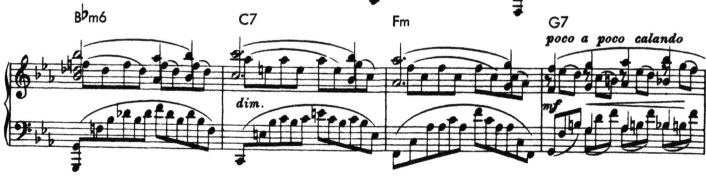

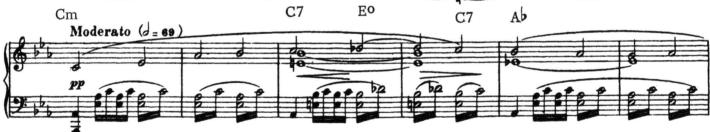

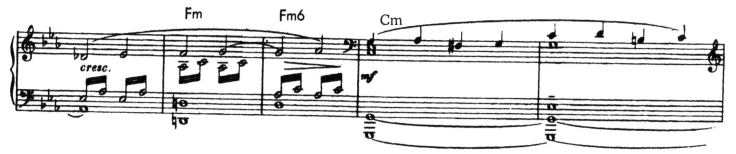

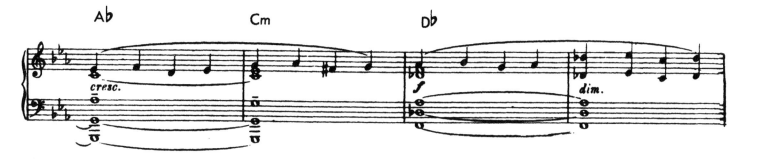

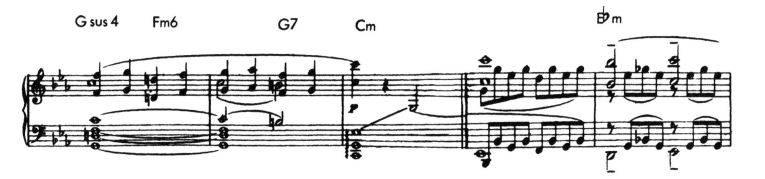

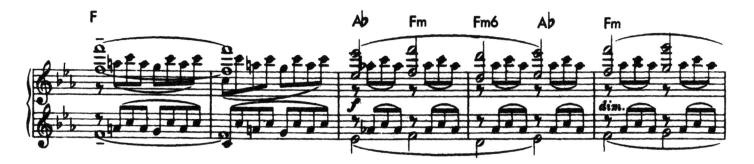

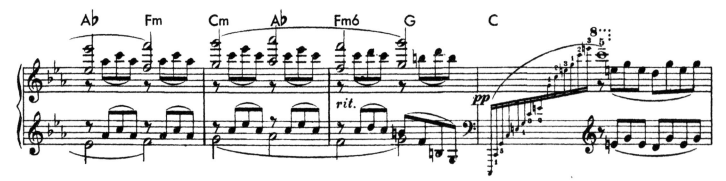

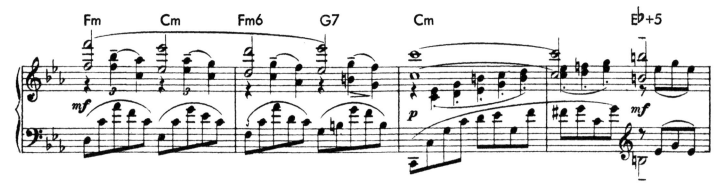

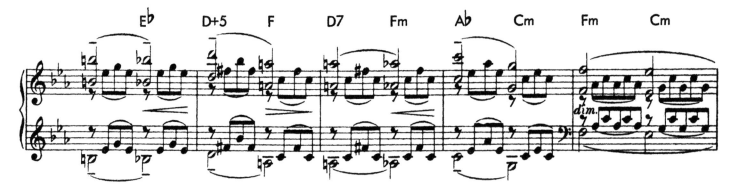

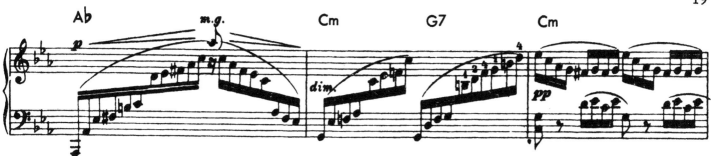

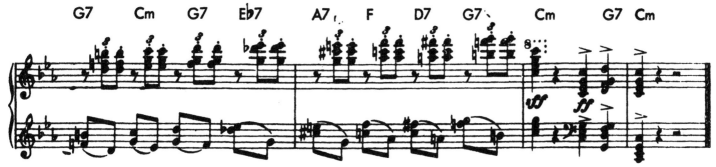

II

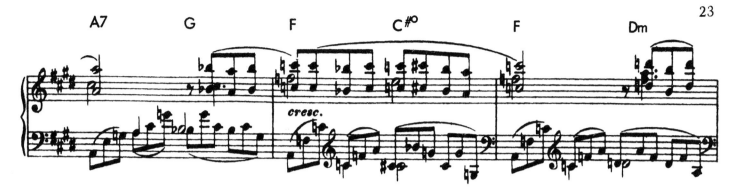

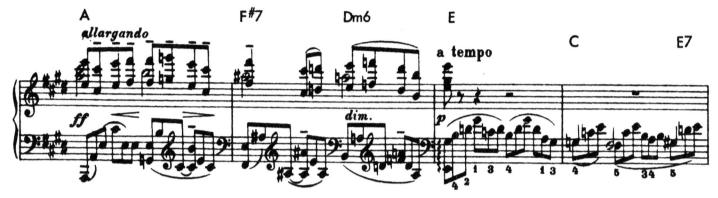

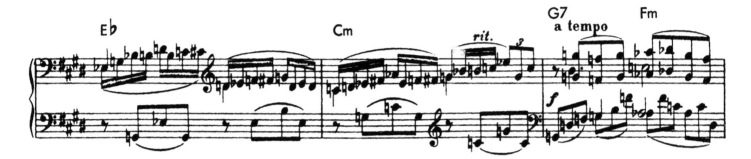

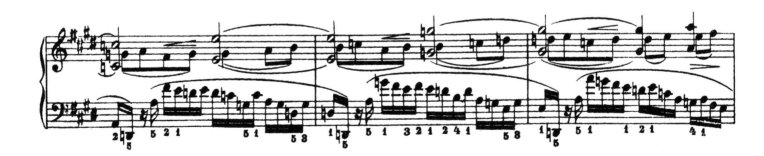

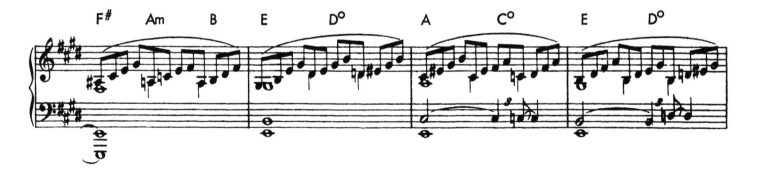

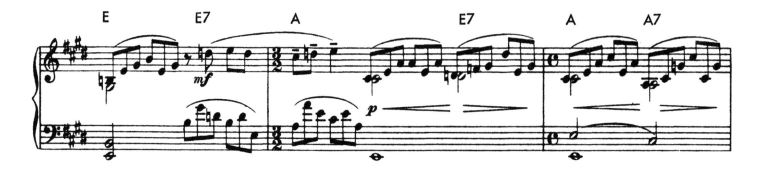

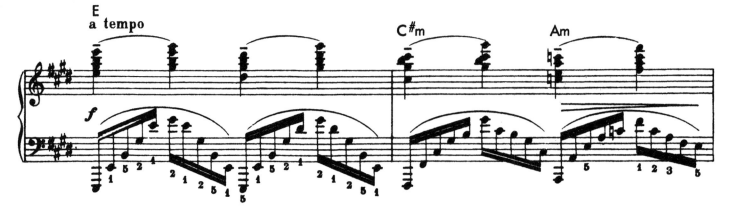

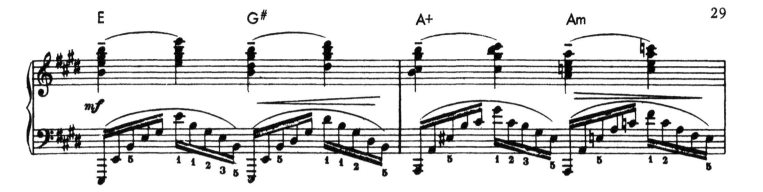

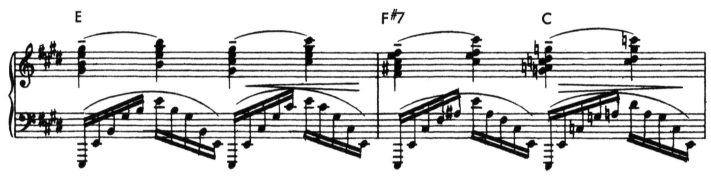

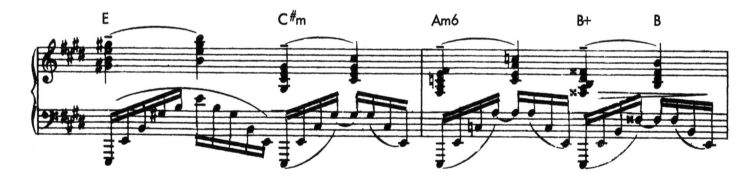

III

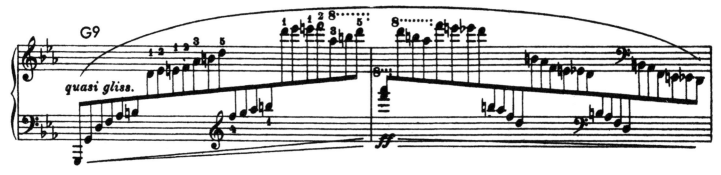

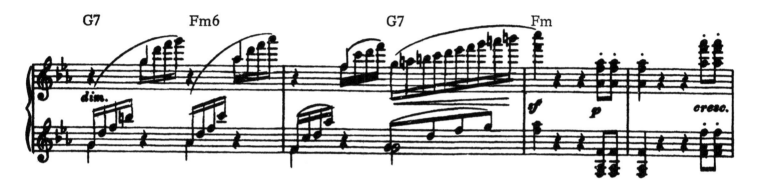

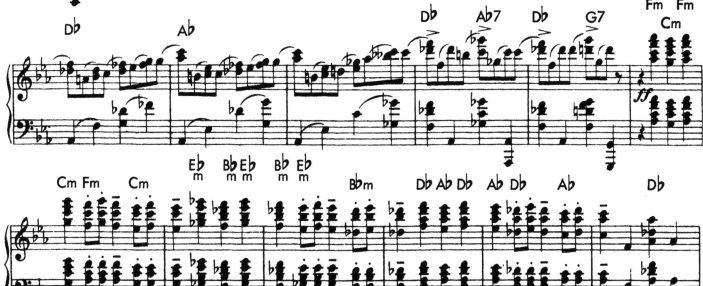

34

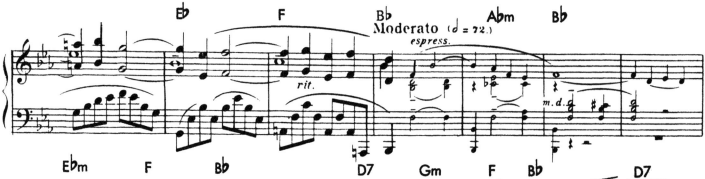

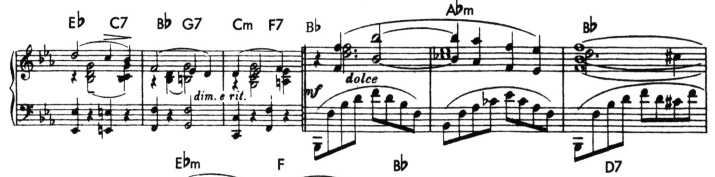

Allegro scherzando (Moto primo.) ($\sddot = 116$.)

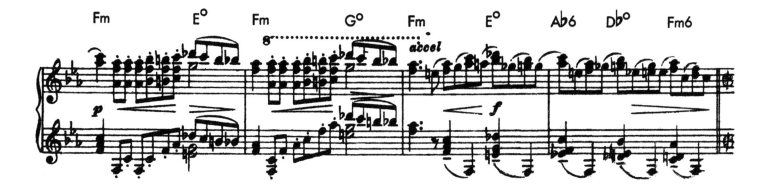

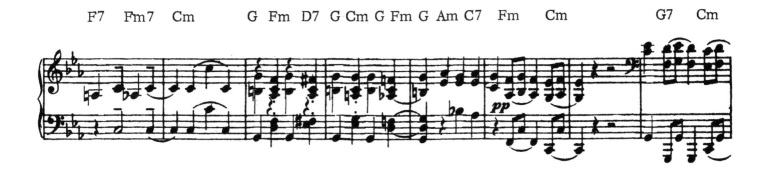

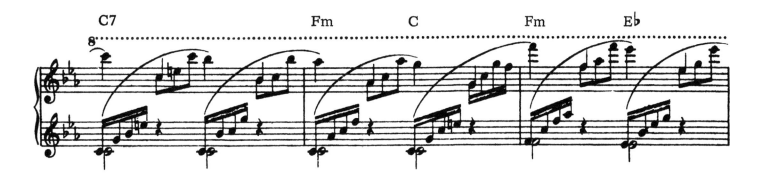

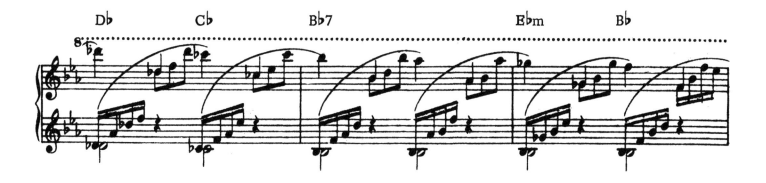

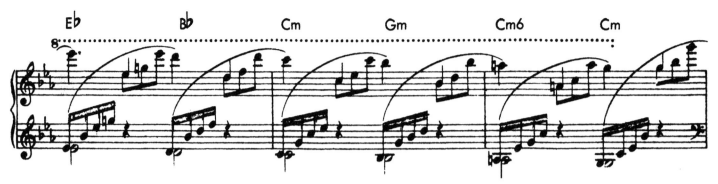

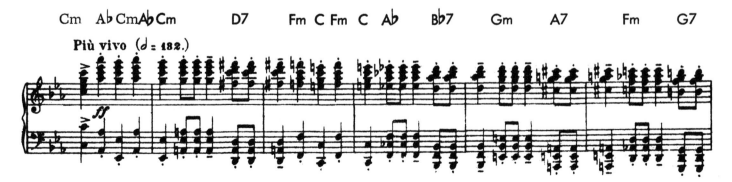

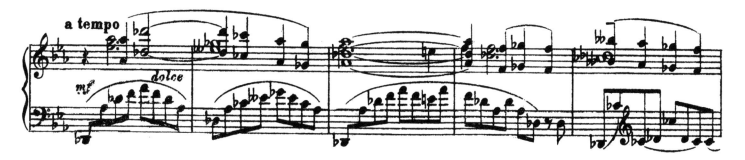

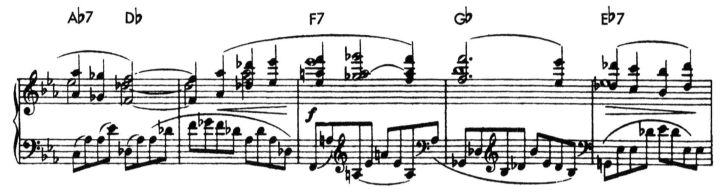

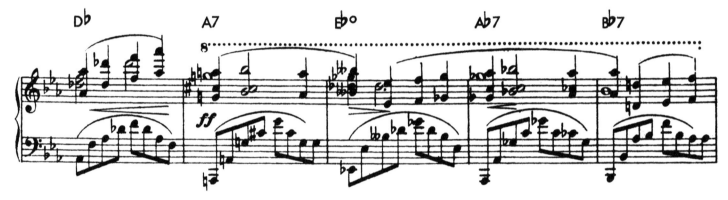

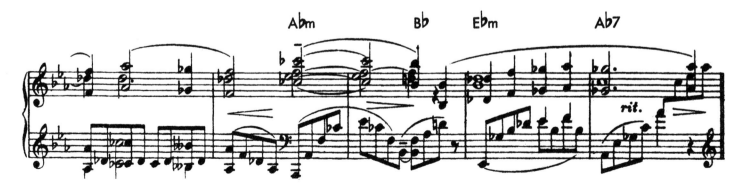

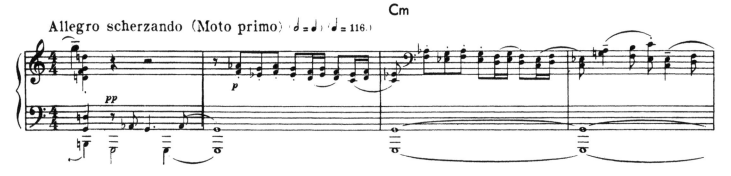

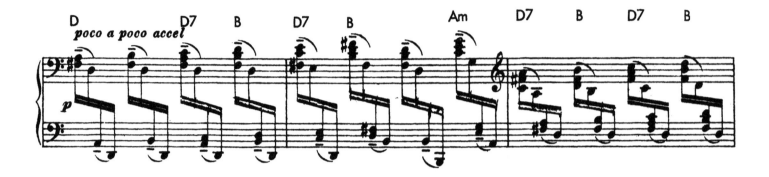

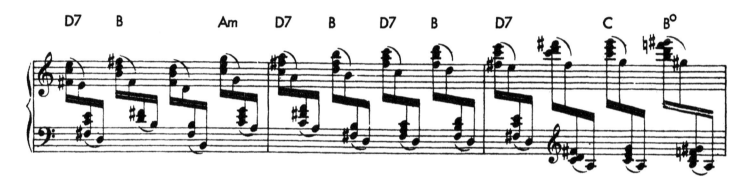

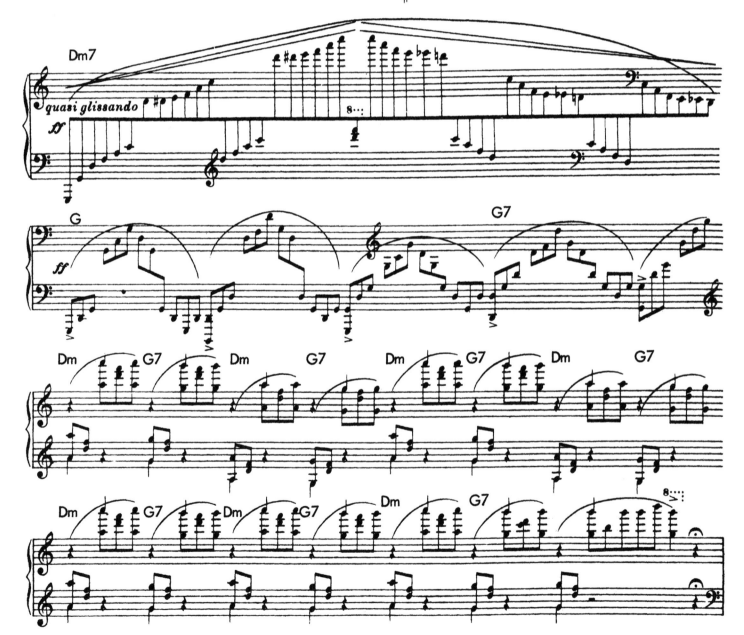

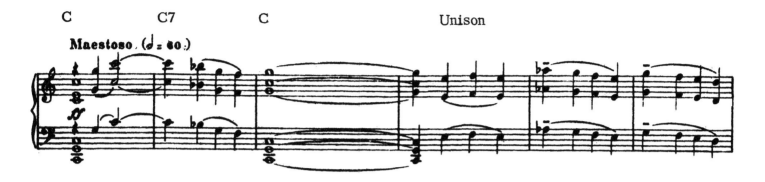

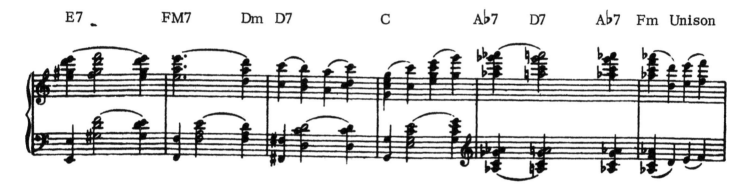

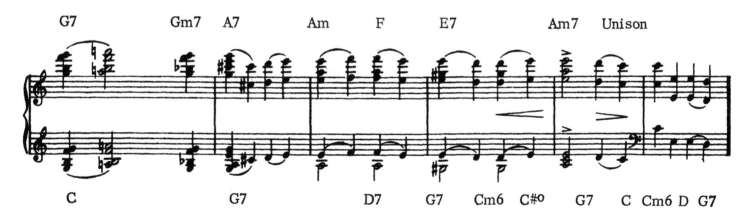

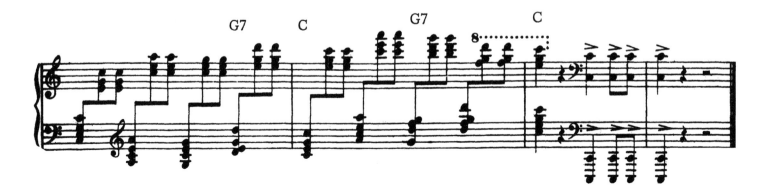